Created and published by Em & Friends
Distributed by Knock Knock Inc.
6695 Green Valley Circle, #5167
Culver City, CA 90230

© 2022 Knock Knock Inc.
All rights reserved
Em & Friends is a trademark of Knock Knock LLC.
Made in China

ISBN: 978-164246-436-8
UPC: 812729029329

10 9 8 7 6 5 4 3 2 1

ONE WORD A DAY

The world's least demanding journal.

EM&FRIENDS

LOS ANGELES, CA

Dear Beautiful, Busy Human Who Aspires to Journal:

Good news! Keeping a journal does not necessarily mean recording every single detail of your dreams, struggles, personal growth, daily activities, random thoughts, or genius observations. It doesn't even have to mean "writing." Not really.

All you need to do to become an official-person-who-journals is just write one word, one teeny-tiny word, that sums up your day. Honestly, it doesn't even have to sum up your whole day—just your dominant feeling about what has most recently happened in your world. Or whatever.

Maybe you want to spend the next 244 days tracking one feeling a day (elation), or perhaps you want to describe what your breakfast tasted like (salty), or what you saw on your morning walk (rainbow) or what took up most of your brain space (bees). You may even want to mix it up—themes aren't mandatory. Future You may look back on this journal years from now and love reading: *Hopeful-ish, Plants, Unicorn, Dumplings, Library*—even if you have no idea what it all means. The biggest takeaway will be: You kept a journal!

If you ever have a day where you can't think of a word, we suggest: PASS or SKIP or even a simple but straightforward NO will do the trick. You don't owe anyone anything, least of all this journal. It's simple. It's poetic. And of course, just one word!

Okay. You get it. Go on ... begin.

DAY 1

In a word:

_____

_ / _ / _

DAY 2

In a
nutshell:

_____

_ / _ / _

DAY 3

Long story short:

_____

_ / _ / _

DAY 4

Succinctly:

_____

_ / _ / _

Concisely put:

_____

_ / _ / _

Just wanna say:

_____

_ / _ / _

DAY 7

In summary:

_____

_ / _ / _

DAY 8

In brief:

_____

_ / _ / _

DAY 9

IYKYK:

_____

_ / _ / _

DAY 10

Today's word:

_____

_ / _ / _

DAY 11

Essentially:

_____

_ / _ / _

DAY 12

It was:

_____

_ / _ / _

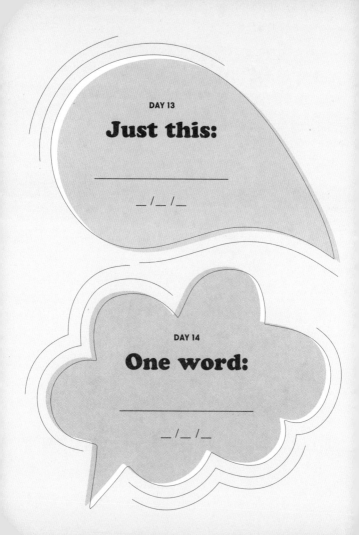

DAY 13

Just this:

_____

_ / _ / _

DAY 14

One word:

_____

_ / _ / _

DAY 15

The word of the day:

_____

_ / _ / _

DAY 16

Basically:

_____

_ / _ / _

In a word:

_____

_ / _ / _

In a nutshell:

_____

_ / _ / _

DAY 19

Long story short:

_____

_ / _ / _

DAY 20

Succinctly:

_____

_ / _ / _

Concisely put:

_____

_ / _ / _

Just wanna say:

_____

_ / _ / _

DAY 23

In summary:

_____

_ / _ / _

DAY 24

In brief:

_____

_ / _ / _

DAY 25

IYKYK:

_____

_ / _ / _

DAY 26

Today's word:

_____

_ / _ / _

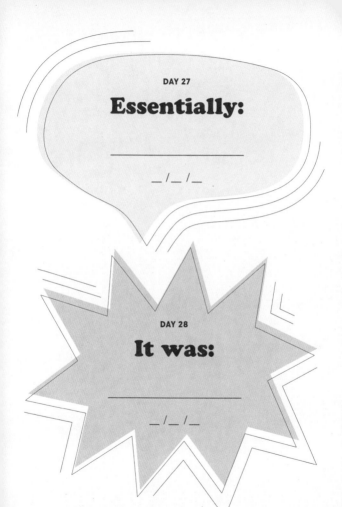

DAY 27

Essentially:

_____

_ / _ / _

DAY 28

It was:

_____

_ / _ / _

DAY 29

Just this:

_____

_ / _ / _

DAY 30

One word:

_____

_ / _ / _

The word of the day:

_____

_ / _ / _

Basically:

_____

_ / _ / _

In a word:

_____

_ / _ / _

In a
nutshell:

_____

_ / _ / _

DAY 35

Long story short:

_____

_ / _ / _

DAY 36

Succinctly:

_____

_ / _ / _

Concisely put:

_____

_ / _ / _

Just wanna say:

_____

_ / _ / _

In summary:

_____

_ / _ / _

In brief:

_____

_ / _ / _

DAY 41

IYKYK:

_____

_ / _ / _

DAY 42

Today's word:

_____

_ / _ / _

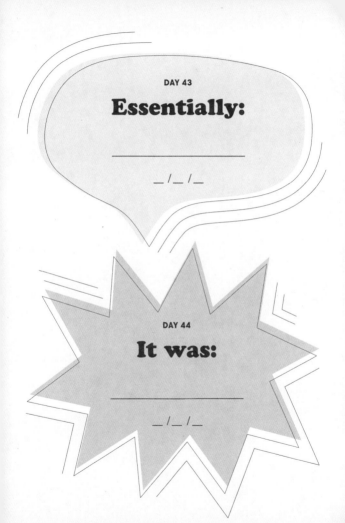

DAY 43

Essentially:

_____

_ / _ / _

DAY 44

It was:

_____

_ / _ / _

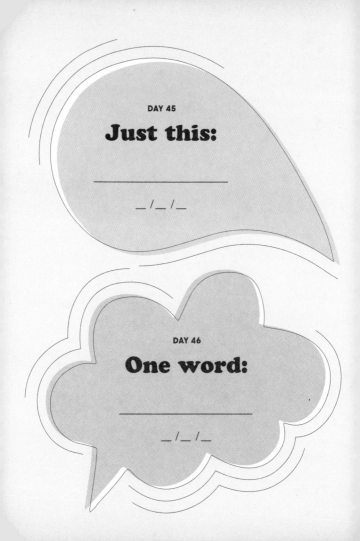

DAY 45

Just this:

_____

_ / _ / _

DAY 46

One word:

_____

_ / _ / _

The word of the day:

_____

_ / _ / _

Basically:

_____

_ / _ / _

In a word:

_____

_ / _ / _

In a nutshell:

_____

_ / _ / _

DAY 51

Long story short:

_____

_ / _ / _

DAY 52

Succinctly:

_____

_ / _ / _

DAY 53

Concisely put:

_____

_ / _ / _

DAY 54

Just wanna say:

_____

_ / _ / _

DAY 55

In summary:

_____

_ / _ / _

DAY 56

In brief:

_____

_ / _ / _

DAY 57

IYKYK:

_____

_ / _ / _

DAY 58

Today's word:

_____

_ / _ / _

DAY 59

Essentially:

_____

_ / _ / _

DAY 60

It was:

_____

_ / _ / _

DAY 61

Just this:

_____

_ / _ / _

DAY 62

One word:

_____

_ / _ / _

DAY 63

The word of the day:

_____

_ / _ / _

DAY 64

Basically:

_____

_ / _ / _

In a word:

_____

_ / _ / _

In a nutshell:

_____

_ / _ / _

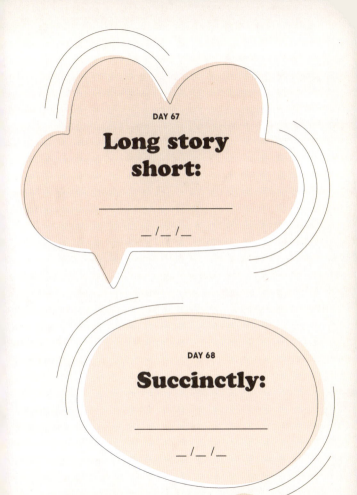

DAY 67

Long story short:

_____

_ / _ / _

DAY 68

Succinctly:

_____

_ / _ / _

DAY 69

Concisely put:

_____

_ / _ / _

DAY 70

Just wanna say:

_____

_ / _ / _

DAY 71

In summary:

_____

_ / _ / _

DAY 72

In brief:

_____

_ / _ / _

DAY 73

IYKYK:

_____

_ / _ / _

DAY 74

Today's word:

_____

_ / _ / _

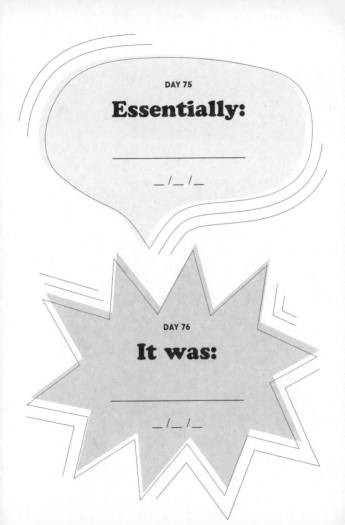

DAY 75

Essentially:

_____

_ / _ / _

DAY 76

It was:

_____

_ / _ / _

DAY 77

Just this:

_____

_ / _ / _

DAY 78

One word:

_____

_ / _ / _

DAY 79

The word of the day:

_____

_ / _ / _

DAY 80

Basically:

_____

_ / _ / _

DAY 81

In a word:

_____

_ / _ / _

DAY 82

In a nutshell:

_____

_ / _ / _

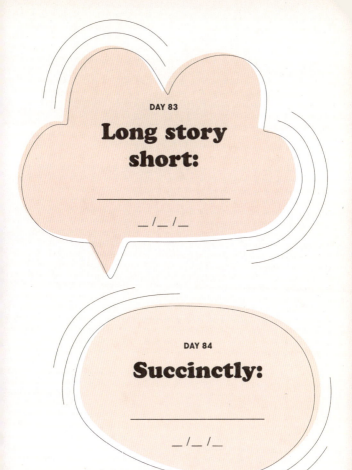

DAY 83

Long story short:

_____

_ / _ / _

DAY 84

Succinctly:

_____

_ / _ / _

Concisely put:

_____

_ / _ / _

Just wanna say:

_____

_ / _ / _

DAY 87

In summary:

_____

_ / _ / _

DAY 88

In brief:

_____

_ / _ / _

DAY 89

IYKYK:

_____

__ / __ / __

DAY 90

Today's word:

_____

__ / __ / __

DAY 91

Essentially:

_____

_ / _ / _

DAY 92

It was:

_____

_ / _ / _

DAY 93

Just this:

_____

__ / __ / __

DAY 94

One word:

_____

__ / __ / __

DAY 95

The word
of the day:

_____

_ / _ / _

DAY 96

Basically:

_____

_ / _ / _

In a word:

_____

_ / _ / _

In a nutshell:

_____

_ / _ / _

DAY 99

Long story short:

_____

_ / _ / _

DAY 100

Succinctly:

_____

_ / _ / _

DAY 101

Concisely put:

_____

_ / _ / _

DAY 102

Just wanna say:

_____

_ / _ / _

DAY 103

In summary:

_____

_ / _ / _

DAY 104

In brief:

_____

_ / _ / _

DAY 105

IYKYK:

_____

_ / _ / _

DAY 106

Today's word:

_____

_ / _ / _

Essentially:

_____

_ / _ / _

It was:

_____

_ / _ / _

DAY 109

Just this:

_____

_ / _ / _

DAY 110

One word:

_____

_ / _ / _

DAY 111

The word
of the day:

_____

_ / _ / _

DAY 112

Basically:

_____

_ / _ / _

In a word:

_____

_ / _ / _

In a nutshell:

_____

_ / _ / _

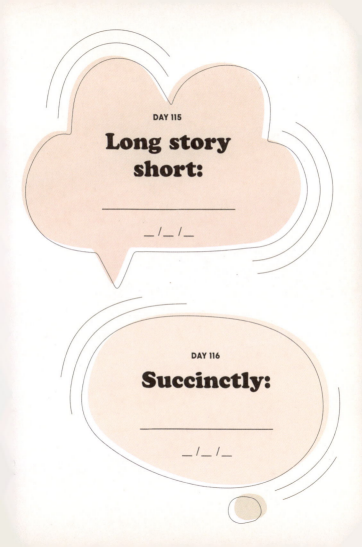

DAY 115

Long story short:

_____

_ / _ / _

DAY 116

Succinctly:

_____

_ / _ / _

Concisely put:

_____

_ / _ / _

Just wanna say:

_____

_ / _ / _

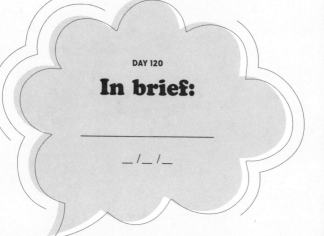

DAY 119

In summary:

_____

_ / _ / _

DAY 120

In brief:

_____

_ / _ / _

DAY 121

IYKYK:

_____

__ / __ / __

DAY 122

Today's word:

_____

__ / __ / __

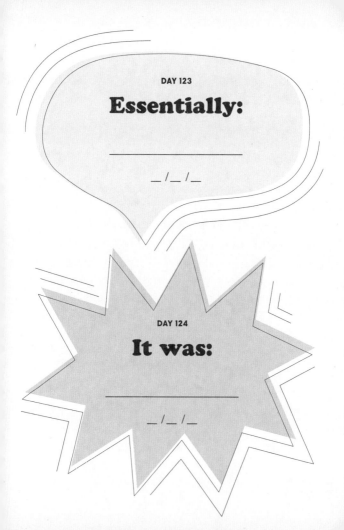

DAY 125

Just this:

_____

_ / _ / _

DAY 126

One word:

_____

_ / _ / _

The word of the day:

_____

_ / _ / _

Basically:

_____

_ / _ / _

DAY 129

In a word:

_____

_ / _ / _

DAY 130

In a
nutshell:

_____

_ / _ / _

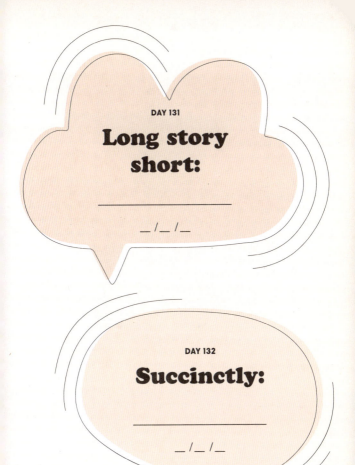

DAY 131

Long story short:

_____

__ / __ / __

DAY 132

Succinctly:

_____

__ / __ / __

Concisely put:

_____

_ / _ / _

Just wanna say:

_____

_ / _ / _

DAY 135

In summary:

_____

_ / _ / _

DAY 136

In brief:

_____

_ / _ / _

DAY 137

IYKYK:

_____

_ / _ / _

DAY 138

Today's word:

_____

_ / _ / _

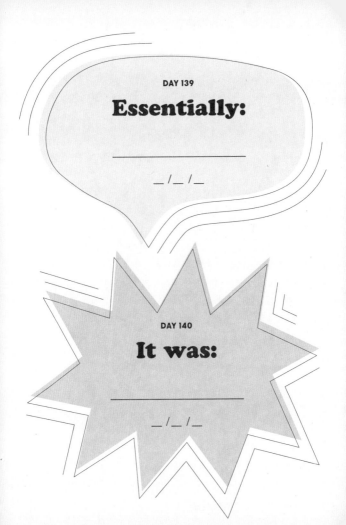

DAY 139

Essentially:

_____

_ / _ / _

DAY 140

It was:

_____

_ / _ / _

DAY 141

Just this:

_____

_ / _ / _

DAY 142

One word:

_____

_ / _ / _

DAY 143

The word
of the day:

_____

_ / _ / _

DAY 144

Basically:

_____

_ / _ / _

DAY 145

In a word:

_____

_ / _ / _

DAY 146

In a nutshell:

_____

_ / _ / _

DAY 147

Long story short:

_____

_ / _ / _

DAY 148

Succinctly:

_____

_ / _ / _

DAY 149

Concisely put:

_____

_ / _ / _

DAY 150

Just wanna say:

_____

_ / _ / _

DAY 151

In summary:

_____

$\_ / \_ / \_$

DAY 152

In brief:

_____

$\_ / \_ / \_$

DAY 153

IYKYK:

_____

__ / __ / __

DAY 154

Today's word:

_____

__ / __ / __

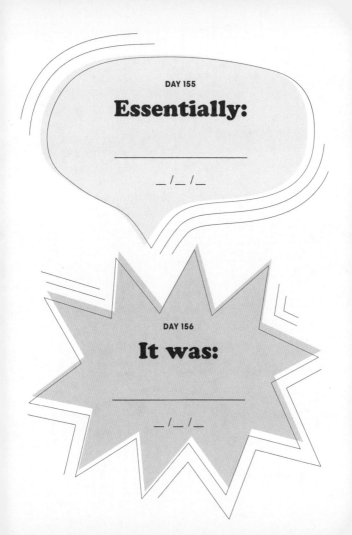

DAY 155

Essentially:

_____

_ / _ / _

DAY 156

It was:

_____

_ / _ / _

DAY 157

Just this:

_____

_ / _ / _

DAY 158

One word:

_____

_ / _ / _

The word
of the day:

_____

_ / _ / _

Basically:

_____

_ / _ / _

In a word:

_____

_ / _ / _

In a nutshell:

_____

_ / _ / _

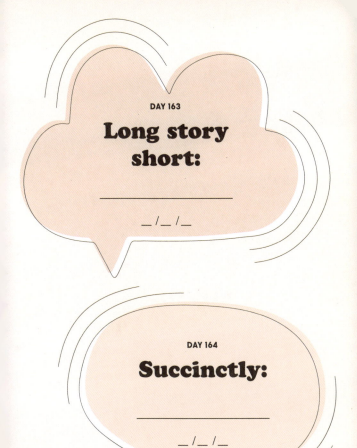

DAY 163

Long story short:

_____

_ / _ / _

DAY 164

Succinctly:

_____

_ / _ / _

Concisely put:

_____

_ / _ / _

Just wanna say:

_____

_ / _ / _

DAY 167

In summary:

_____

_ / _ / _

DAY 168

In brief:

_____

_ / _ / _

DAY 169

IYKYK:

_____

_ / _ / _

DAY 170

Today's word:

_____

_ / _ / _

DAY 171

Essentially:

_____

_ / _ / _

DAY 172

It was:

_____

_ / _ / _

DAY 173

Just this:

_____

_ / _ / _

DAY 174

One word:

_____

_ / _ / _

The word of the day:

_____

_ / _ / _

Basically:

_____

_ / _ / _

In a word:

_____

_ / _ / _

In a nutshell:

_____

_ / _ / _

Long story short:

_____

_ / _ / _

Succinctly:

_____

_ / _ / _

Concisely put:

_____

_ / _ / _

Just wanna say:

_____

_ / _ / _

DAY 183

In summary:

_____

_ / _ / _

DAY 184

In brief:

_____

_ / _ / _

DAY 185

IYKYK:

_____

_ / _ / _

DAY 186

Today's word:

_____

_ / _ / _

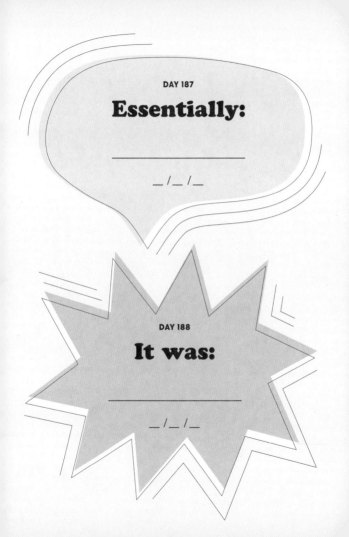

DAY 187

Essentially:

_____

_ / _ / _

DAY 188

It was:

_____

_ / _ / _

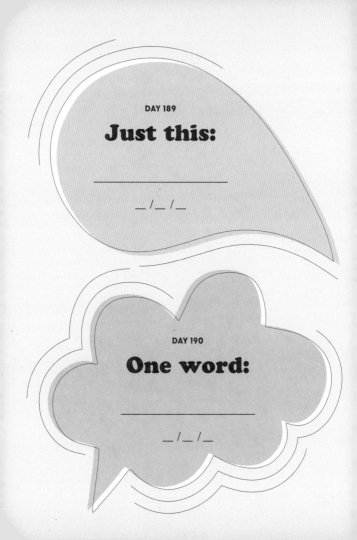

DAY 189

Just this:

_____

_ / _ / _

DAY 190

One word:

_____

_ / _ / _

The word of the day:

_____

_ / _ / _

Basically:

_____

_ / _ / _

In a word:

_____

_ / _ / _

In a nutshell:

_____

_ / _ / _

DAY 195

Long story short:

_____

_ / _ / _

DAY 196

Succinctly:

_____

_ / _ / _

Concisely put:

_____

_ / _ / _

Just wanna say:

_____

_ / _ / _

DAY 199

In summary:

_____

_ / _ / _

DAY 200

In brief:

_____

_ / _ / _

DAY 201

IYKYK:

_____

_ / _ / _

DAY 202

Today's word:

_____

_ / _ / _

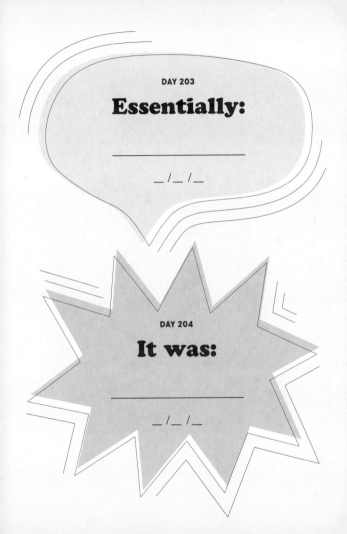

DAY 203

Essentially:

_____

_ / _ / _

DAY 204

It was:

_____

_ / _ / _

DAY 205

Just this:

_____

_ / _ / _

DAY 206

One word:

_____

_ / _ / _

The word
of the day:

_____

_ / _ / _

Basically:

_____

_ / _ / _

In a word:

_____

_ / _ / _

In a nutshell:

_____

_ / _ / _

Long story short:

_____

_ / _ / _

Succinctly:

_____

_ / _ / _

DAY 213

Concisely put:

_____

_ / _ / _

DAY 214

Just wanna say:

_____

_ / _ / _

DAY 215

In summary:

_____

_ / _ / _

DAY 216

In brief:

_____

_ / _ / _

DAY 217

IYKYK:

_____

_ / _ / _

DAY 218

Today's word:

_____

_ / _ / _

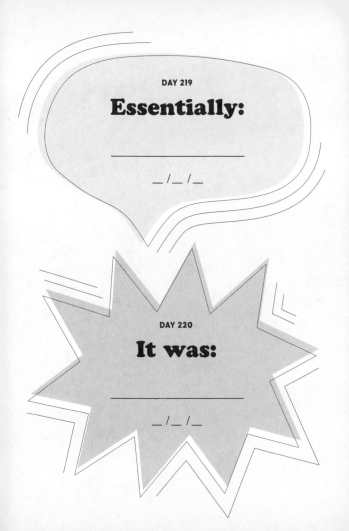

DAY 219

Essentially:

_____

_ / _ / _

DAY 220

It was:

_____

_ / _ / _

DAY 221

Just this:

_____

_ / _ / _

DAY 222

One word:

_____

_ / _ / _

The word of the day:

_____

_ / _ / _

Basically:

_____

_ / _ / _

In a word:

_____

_ / _ / _

In a
nutshell:

_____

_ / _ / _

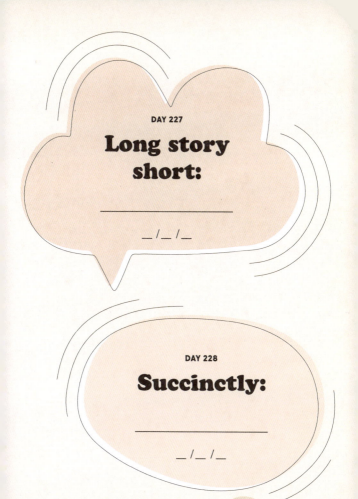

DAY 227

Long story short:

_____

_ / _ / _

DAY 228

Succinctly:

_____

_ / _ / _

Concisely put:

_____

_ / _ / _

Just wanna say:

_____

_ / _ / _

DAY 231

In summary:

_____

_ / _ / _

DAY 232

In brief:

_____

_ / _ / _

DAY 233

IYKYK:

_____

_ / _ / _

DAY 234

Today's word:

_____

_ / _ / _

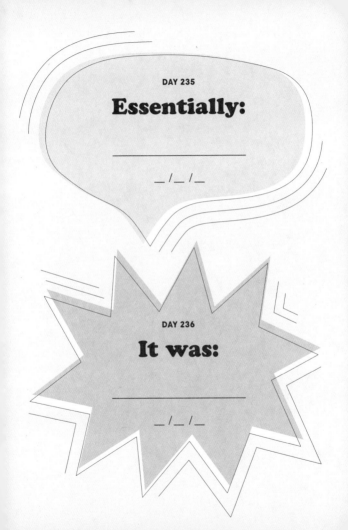

DAY 235

Essentially:

_____

_ / _ / _

DAY 236

It was:

_____

_ / _ / _

DAY 237

Just this:

_____

_ / _ / _

DAY 238

One word:

_____

_ / _ / _

The word of the day:

_____

_ / _ / _

Basically:

_____

_ / _ / _

In a word:

————————————

_ / _ / _

In a nutshell:

————————————

_ / _ / _

DAY 243

Long story short:

_____

_ / _ / _

DAY 244

Succinctly:

_____

_ / _ / _